Survivors
On the Rock Face

John Goodwin

Published in association with
The Basic Skills Agency

Hodder Murray
A MEMBER OF THE HODDER HEADLINE GROUP

The Publishers would like to thank the following for permisson to reproduce copyright material:

Photo Credits
pp. 3, 7 © James Osmond / Alamy

Orders: please contact Bookpoint Ltd, 130 Milton Park, Abingdon, Oxon OX14 4SB. Telephone: (44) 01235 827720. Fax: (44) 01235 400454. Lines are open 9.00–6.00, Monday to Saturday, with a 24-hour message answering service. Visit our website at www.hoddereducation.co.uk

Impression number   10 9 8 7 6 5 4 3 2 1
Year   2010 2009 2008 2007 2006 2005

Cover photo © James Osmond / Alamy.
Illustrations by Gary Andrews.
Typeset by Transet Limited, Coventry, England.
Printed in Great Britain by Athenaeum Press Ltd, Gateshead, Tyne & Wear.

A catalogue record for this title is available from the British Library

ISBN-10: 0 340 90066 0
ISBN-13: 978 0 340 90066 6

Contents

1

'Your turn, Fleahead,'
said Watson the instructor.
I turned towards him and my mouth fell open.
Everybody started to giggle
for the tenth time that morning.
'What planet are you on, Fleahead?' barked
Watson.
'This is a survivors' course, not a picnic.'

OK, Watson. You've had your cheap laughs.
My name is Harry.
Harry.
It's a short enough name, isn't it?
So why can't you use it?

I looked up at the high rock face.
It rose steeply above my head.
Even looking up made me feel dizzy and sick.

I'm scared of heights.
But I don't want anyone to know it.

On the Survivors' Course
you have to hide your feelings.
I say to myself, 'Don't let it get to you.'
Over and over again.
The rock face was smooth.
There were a few small holds.
Thin cracks to grip with your hands.
Little ledges to press your feet into.
But it wasn't easy.

My confidence had collapsed quicker than
water empties out of a washing machine
on a fast spin.

Watson fastened the rope into my harness.
Clunk went the karabiner snap link.
Panic filled my heart.
Shake and shake again went my legs.
'Don't dither, Fleahead,' said Watson,
taking hold of his end of the rope.
'You're holding everybody up.'

I took half a step forward.
Then I stopped.
Behind me, Jez started to make chicken noises.
'Fleas can't climb rocks.
Their grubby little feet
can't reach the holds,' he shouted.

Jez, Lucy and Tariq started to laugh.
Even Ben was giggling
and he's supposed to be my best mate.
'I make the jokes, Jez,' shouted Watson
in a very loud voice.

'You're here to learn.
If you want to survive this course,
you'd best remember that.'

'Maybe I'll wait for a bit,' I said.
'Let somebody else go next.'
Jez ran forward.
'Me … I'll do it,' he said,
reaching out to grab the rope.
But Watson blocked his way.
'No,' he barked.
'Fleahead has three more seconds
to move himself.'

I took a deep breath
and another half-step forward.
I had to give it a try.
'I'm climbing,' I said.
I quickly stepped close to the rock.
I reached up for the first handhold.
It was easy to grip.
With my hand gripping the hold, I could step up.
I put my foot on to a lump in the rock.
I pushed hard on my foot.

Then my left foot came off the ground.
Brilliant.
I was off the ground.
My climb had really begun.
The next few moves were easy.
The hand and footholds were close together.
I was making good progress up the rock.
As long as I didn't look down, I was OK.

Maybe it wasn't going to be so bad after all.
Even fleas have their good days, don't they?
Up and up I climbed.
I began to enjoy the excitement.
The buzz of it all.

Then I got stuck.
The next handhold above me
was way out of my reach.
I was standing on a small sloping ledge.
I tried to stretch up with my right hand
as high as I could.
But it was no use.
I still couldn't reach the next hold.

Then I made a big mistake.
I looked down to the ground below me.
Beneath my feet,
a big black space opened up.
I was stuck halfway up the rock face.
I couldn't move up or down.
Everyone was just waiting for me to fail.

My legs began to tremble and shake.
Everyone could see what a mess I was in.
'Told you he was too small,'
shouted Jez down on the ground.
'He'll never do it.'

Harry—

Panic came over my whole body.
My shaking foot slipped off the small ledge.
I couldn't hold on with my hands.

Off the rock I fell.
Watson took my weight on the rope.
I slithered down very, very slowly.
Everybody booed and then they laughed.

2

I went to my room in the Activity Centre.
I tried to chill out by myself.
My mobile rang.
Jez had sent me a text.

```
ru chickn or man?
```

Then there was a second text message.
This one was from Lucy.

```
u loozer
```

Thanks, Lucy.

Just what I needed.

I switched off my mobile and had a shower.
At least that would chill me out.

When I came out of the shower,
I dried myself in a big towel.
Then I went to put my clothes back on.
No clothes.
I looked on the bed where I'd left them.
I looked under the bed.
No clothes anywhere.

I searched in the rucksack
I'd brought with me.
I opened every drawer and cupboard.
All my clothes had disappeared.

I lost my cool.
I hit the wall with my fist
and I kicked out at my bed.
It didn't help.
My big toe hurt and my fist ached.

Seconds ticked by.
It had to be Jez and Lucy.
They must have come into my room
when I was in the shower.

What was I going to do?
Walk around the Centre in a towel
looking for them?
No way.
I'd had enough pain for one day.

I sat on my bed for ages and did nothing.
I looked at my mobile.
Maybe I could text Ben.
Maybe not.
He'd only think I was pathetic.

It was getting close to meal-time.
I switched on my mobile.
I sent a text to Ben.

```
can u help me? cum to my room
```

Ben came straight away.
Then he found Lucy.
My clothes were hidden in the laundry room.
Lucy brought them all back.
'It was only a joke, Harry.
Just a bit of a laugh. OK?'

No, it's not OK.
It's never been OK.

3

Survivors
Tomorrow
is Abseil day.
Meet at 9am sharp
at the rock face.

My heart thumped.
An abseil is where you have to lower yourself
down from the top of the rock face
on a rope.
How could I lower myself down
when I couldn't climb up it?

I'd failed the rock climbing.
If I failed the abseil too,
I'd be in big trouble.
I'd have to do extra work
at it every single night.
While everyone else was lazing about,
I'd be sweating away.
To fail one challenge is OK,
but you can't fail two.

Ben was looking at Watson's abseil notice.
'That will be a laugh,' he said.
Then he saw my face.
'Or maybe it won't,' he added.
'I'll never do it,' I said.
'I'll just make an idiot of myself again.
Then everybody can boo.'

It went quiet for a while, and then Ben said,
'What if we could have a look at it first?
There's an easy path behind the rock
that takes you right to the top of it.
Why don't we go there?'
'Now?' I asked.

'Meet me outside in the car park
in ten minutes,' he said.
'There's something I have to do first.'

Ten minutes later I was waiting
in the car park alone.
There was no sign of Ben.
Then he came out of the building
carrying his rucksack.
'What have you got in there?' I asked.
He didn't answer,
but he began to jog off towards the rock.
'Just follow me,' he said.

4

We came to wide open moorland
where our path divided.
'If we go down, we'll be
at the bottom of the rock,' said Ben.
'So we want to take this higher path.'
Off he jogged again, and I followed.

The ground was steep,
but we soon stood at the top of the rock.
I looked down on to the rock face.

From up there it didn't seem so scary.
There wasn't anyone around to jeer or boo.
It was so quiet.
Maybe I could abseil down it.

I turned to see Ben opening up his rucksack.
He pulled a big loop of rope out of it.
'Where did you get that from?'
'I thought we'd have a practice
before tomorrow,' he explained.
'Just the two of us.'

'Oh no you don't,' said a voice
that wasn't mine.
We looked round to see Watson,
glaring at us both.
'Stealing our rope is bad enough,' he said.
'But coming here without any adults
is breaking all the rules.
What do you think you're doing?'

We tried to explain,
but Watson didn't want to listen.
He banned us going out at night
for a whole week.
We also had to get up early each morning
to do an hour's workout in the gym.

5

Watson pushed himself out
from the top of the rock face.
His body was suspended in mid-air.
Below him there was a huge black gap.
The ground beneath his body
was way, way below.
Only the flat underneath of his boots
had any contact with the rock.

Yet he was in perfect control.
A rope loop ran through his safety karabiner.
It was fastened around a giant iron spike
at the top of the rock.
He held his body completely still and smiled.
'Easy as eating your dinner,' he said.
'Perfectly safe. Just a bit of fun.
Relax. Enjoy.'

Watson smiled again.
'You'll all do this perfectly first time.
Even you, Fleahead.'

His body then fell at speed down the rock.
It looked like he was going to crash
into the ground.
Surely he'd smash every bone in his body.
Then he touched the brake
on his safety harness.

Immediately he came to a complete stop.
He was only centimetres from the ground.
His loud laugh echoed up to us all
at the top of the rock.

Lucy started to clap her hands.
Most of the group joined in.
'Brilliant,' she shouted.
'Top shot,' cried Jez.
'Wicked,' screamed Tariq.

I just thought, 'Why are you such a poser?
Isn't it time you grew up?'

6

Watson climbed back up the rock in seconds.
Then he turned to us all.
'Right, who's first?' he said.

Everybody was silent.
Lucy took a step backwards.
Tariq looked down to the ground way below.
Jez bent down to fiddle with his laces.
Ben looked away.

'Come on,' said Watson.
'It's a piece of cake.
A Sunday stroll.'
Then he stared at me.
'What about you Fleahead?
To show you're more man than chicken?'

The booing started again.
So did the laughing.
Everyone was looking at me.
Lucy started to do a slow handclap.

I couldn't take any more.
It was either run or bust.
'OK. I'll do it,' I said.
It went quiet.
'You don't have to,' said Ben.
'Oh yes I do,' said a voice in my head.

Before I could stop myself,
I took a step nearer the edge of the rock.
'Tie me on,' I said.

Watson put the safety harness on me.
He threaded a second safety rope
around the spike.
A length of the rope was thrown down
to the bottom of the rock.
But it got tangled up in a knot.
He had to haul it back to the top
and do it again.

Why was it taking so long?
I just wanted to do it quickly.

No more waiting.
I could hardly breathe.
Ben tried to crack a joke
to help me relax.
Make me laugh.
'Shut up, Ben,' I thought.
It was making me feel worse.

I wanted it done with.
Ended.
To be standing on the ground below in safety.
Not shaking.

I tried to think of the text messages
I might get if I did it.

```
    wot  a  *
```

```
ur  a  survivor,  Harry
```

At last Watson fixed the ropes.
I looked right over the edge.
Couldn't I change my mind?
How could I have been so stupid, going first?
My boots scrabbled
on the very edge of the rock.

'Lower your body and keep your legs stiff,'
said Watson.
How could I make my legs stiff
when they were shaking like a jelly?
'Take your weight on the rope
and push yourself out.'

Nothing below me but wide empty space.
How far down?
Head dizzy.
Senses swimming.

I closed my eyes and kept them shut tight.
I tried to push myself out.
'That's it … That's it.
You're doing it.'

I felt myself
start to slither down the rope.
But my legs weren't following.
'Your legs ... Move your legs down.'

I slithered some more
but still my legs were stuck at the top.
'He's hanging upside down,'
yelled a girl's voice.
Then giggling and laughing.

Someone pushed my legs free
and they shot down the rock face.
The pain of it all forced me to open my eyes.
Then I slithered and slid, and stumbled
slowly down to the bottom.
I landed on the ground softly.

Silence.
Then a cheer broke out.
Someone was clapping.
'You did it, Harry,' shouted Ben.
I looked round at the ground
and up to the top of the rock.

Did I really do it?
Everyone was smiling.
I'd survived.